Continents

Europe

GALADRIEL WATSON

MEDIA ENHANCED BOOKS

AV2 BY WEIGL™

ADDED VALUE · AUDIO VISUAL

www.av2books.com

AV² provides enriched content that supplements and complements this book. Weigl's AV² books strive to create inspired learning and engage young minds in a total learning experience.

Your AV² Media Enhanced books come alive with...

Audio
Listen to sections of the book read aloud.

Key Words
Study vocabulary, and complete a matching word activity.

Go to **www.av2books.com**, and enter this book's unique code.

Video
Watch informative video clips.

Quizzes
Test your knowledge.

BOOK CODE

T139045

Embedded Weblinks
Gain additional information for research.

Slide Show
View images and captions, and prepare a presentation.

AV² by Weigl brings you media enhanced books that support active learning.

Try This!
Complete activities and hands-on experiments.

... and much, much more!

Published by AV² by Weigl
350 5th Avenue, 59th Floor
New York, NY 10118
Website: www.av2books.com   www.weigl.com

Library of Congress Cataloging-in-Publication Data

Watson, Galadriel Findlay.
 Europe / Galadriel Watson.
    p. cm. — (Continents)
 Includes index.
 ISBN 978-1-61913-447-8 (hard cover : alk. paper) — ISBN 978-1-61913-448-5 (soft cover : alk. paper)
 1. Europe—Juvenile literature. I. Title.
 D1051.W27 2013
 940—dc23
                             2011051208

Printed in the United States of America in North Mankato, Minnesota
2 3 4 5 6 7 8 9 0 16 15 14 13 12

112012
WEP081112

Project Coordinator Karen Durrie
Art Director Terry Paulhus

Photo Credits
Every reasonable effort has been made to trace ownership and to obtain permission to reprint copyright material. The publishers would be pleased to have any errors or omissions brought to their attention so that they may be corrected in subsequent printings.

Weigl acknowledges Getty Images as its primary image supplier for this title.

Continents

Europe

Contents

Introduction

Europe covers an area of nearly 4 million square miles (10.4 million square kilometers), or about 7 percent of Earth's land. Its land area is smaller than most other continents. Europe makes up in **diversity**, however, what it lacks in size.

Europe's warm coastal waters attract millions of swimmers and sunbathers each year, while skiers and climbers adore the continent's high mountain peaks. Europe has modern cities and open fields of wheat, oats, and sunflowers. Glittering glass skyscrapers stand not far from crumbling **medieval** castles.

European peoples have played very important roles throughout world history. Their influence on arts, science, politics, philosophy, and religion dates as far back as 3000 BC. European efforts to explore new lands and develop new trade routes led to the creation of many countries, from Canada and the United States to Australia and South Africa.

The "Beefeater" uniform worn by guards at the Tower of London is one of Great Britain's most familiar symbols.

Europe is generally considered to have 45 countries. Most lie wholly within Europe. A few others are located partly in Europe and partly in Asia. The western region of Russia is considered part of Europe, while eastern Russia belongs to Asia. At nearly twice the size of the United States, Russia is the largest country in the world. Russia's capital city, Moscow, is located on the European continent and ranks among Europe's largest cities. Other major countries of Europe include Germany, France, Great Britain, and Italy.

Vatican City is Europe's, and the world's, smallest country. Surrounded by the Italian city of Rome, Vatican City covers only 0.17 square miles (0.44 sq km). Also known as the Holy See, Vatican City is the headquarters of the Catholic Church. The city is home to the pope, who heads the Catholic Church and also holds the title of bishop of Rome. The city's total population is less than 1,000.

The onion-shaped domes of Saint Basil's Cathedral in Moscow are a well-known Russian landmark.

Europe

Europe is located in the Northern Hemisphere. Its northern boundary is the Arctic Ocean. It is bordered on the west by the Atlantic Ocean. The Mediterranean Sea, the Black Sea, and the Caucasus Mountains border Europe to the south.

Europe's eastern boundary is difficult to determine. On its east side, Europe is attached to the continent of Asia. Some geographers believe Europe and Asia should not be considered two separate continents. They believe Europe and Asia are part of a larger continent called Eurasia. Other geographers believe Europe is a distinct continent. Many of these geographers agree that the boundary between Europe and Asia includes the Ural Mountains, the Ural River, and the Caspian Sea.

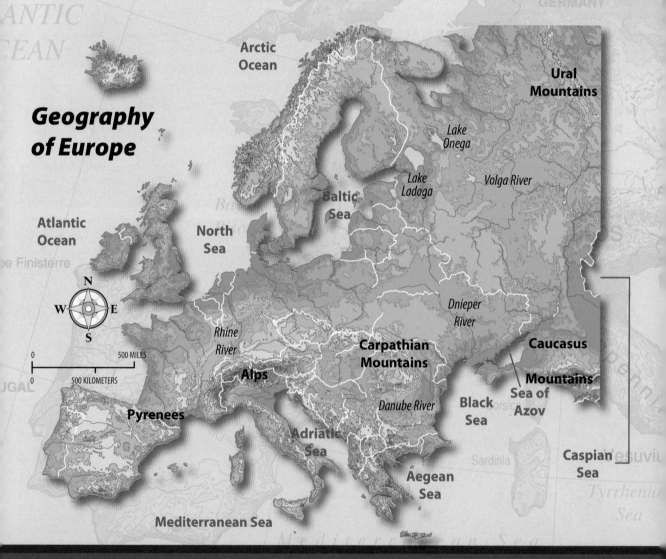

Geography of Europe

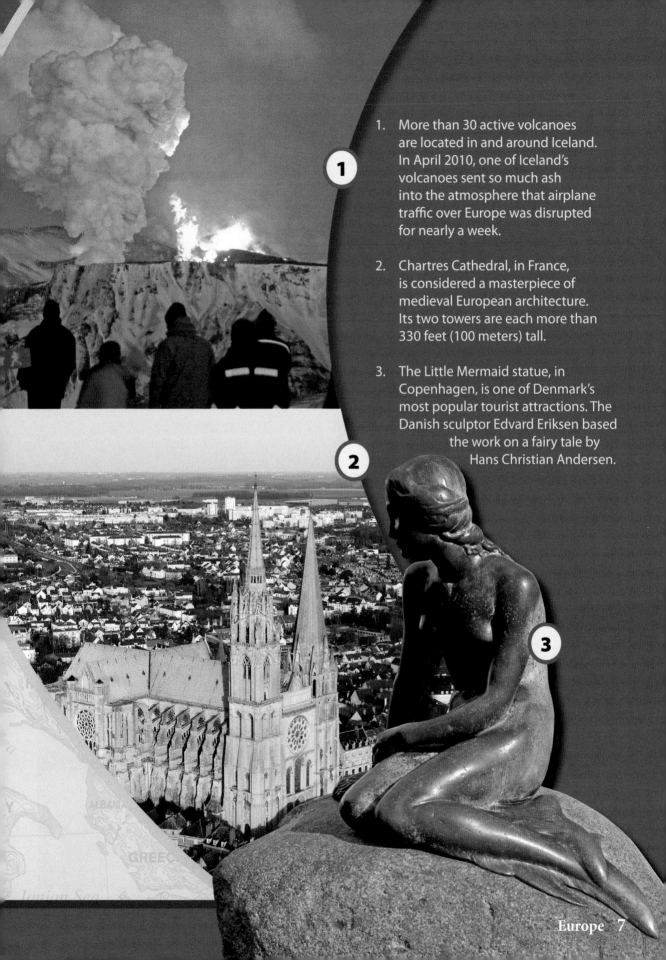

1 1. More than 30 active volcanoes are located in and around Iceland. In April 2010, one of Iceland's volcanoes sent so much ash into the atmosphere that airplane traffic over Europe was disrupted for nearly a week.

2. Chartres Cathedral, in France, is considered a masterpiece of medieval European architecture. Its two towers are each more than 330 feet (100 meters) tall.

3. The Little Mermaid statue, in Copenhagen, is one of Denmark's most popular tourist attractions. The Danish sculptor Edvard Eriksen based the work on a fairy tale by Hans Christian Andersen.

Land and Climate

Europe can be divided into four main geographic regions. These four major regions are the Northwest Mountains, the Great European Plain, the Central Uplands, and the Alpine Mountains. Most of these areas are populated. Only a few places, such as in the extreme north or on mountaintops, are unable to support life.

In the Northwest Mountains, the mountains are so old that most have worn down. The Great European Plain in the south and in Russia offers some of the world's best farmland and is home to many of Europe's residents. The Central Uplands consist of low mountains and large **plateaus**. Finally, several mountain chains cross southern Europe. These mountains include the Alps, the Pyrenees, and the Caucasus.

Much of Poland lies within the Great European Plain. Farms cover about 40 percent of the nation's land area.

The Pyrenees Mountains straddle the border between France and Spain.

Much of the European continent has mild weather. Winds blow across the Atlantic Ocean, where the Gulf Stream current warms them. These warm winds sweep across the continent, generally keeping the land at moderate temperatures. Most European countries have four seasons. In these countries, winter occurs between November and March. Summer takes place between June and September.

In general, areas in the northern and eastern parts of the continent have longer, colder winters and shorter, cooler summers than places in the south or west. Northern Europe has the coldest climates on the continent. In some northern regions, during the bitter winter months, there is little or no daylight. In the summer, however, the Sun shines 24 hours per day. Central Europe has overcast, rainy winters with moderate summers. In the southern part of Europe, the summers are hot, and the winters are mild with little rain.

Helsinki, Finland, is one of the coldest capital cities in Europe. The city's year-round temperature averages about 40° Fahrenheit (4.4° Celsius).

Get This!

Europe's highest mountain is Mount Elbrus in Russia. It rises 18,510 feet (5,642 m) above sea level.

Europe's longest river is the Volga River. It flows 2,290 miles (3,685 km) from Russia to the Caspian Sea.

Geographers believe Europe and the other continents once belonged to a huge landmass called Pangaea. Over time, this giant continent broke apart. Europe took its current shape about 5 million years ago.

Plants and Animals

E urope's plant life is found in three zones: forests, grasslands, and **tundra**. Although many European forests have been cut down, large forested areas still exist in northern countries and in Russia. Smaller patches of woodland are located farther south. Olive and cork oak trees grow along the Mediterranean coast. European grasslands include prairies and **steppes**. Tundra areas and mountain peaks are cold and without trees. Plant life in these treeless regions includes small shrubs, wildflowers, and lichens.

Most large European animals thrive only in wildlife reserves or in places that are difficult for people to reach. Reindeer live in Europe's cold tundra regions. Other tundra animals include the Arctic fox and snowy owl. Animals in Europe's forests include wolves, elks, and European brown bears. Wild boars live near the Mediterranean Sea.

Europe has many small animals, such as rabbits, squirrels, badgers, hedgehogs, moles, and lemmings. Rodents, such as marmots and field mice, live in the continent's grassland areas, as do many kinds of birds and insects. Seals and fish, such as anchovy, cod, salmon, and tuna, live in Europe's coastal waters.

The lady's-slipper orchid is one of Europe's **endangered** plant species.

At one time, forests covered about 80 percent of Europe. They now cover about one-third of Europe's land area.

Europe's largest mammal is the European bison. Prehistoric cave drawings in Europe show bison, along with **extinct** animals such as aurochs, or long-horned wild oxen. At one time, Europe was also home to elephants and wild horses.

A European brown bear can weigh up to 1,500 pounds (680 kilograms).

Natural Resources

Europeans enjoy many natural advantages. For example, Europe has some of the world's best farmland. About one-fourth of the continent is covered with farms. Much of Europe's cropland is used to grow grains such as barley, oats, and wheat. More than 90 percent of the world's rye comes from Europe. Other farmers raise livestock, such as sheep, cattle, and pigs. Fishing is important in many European countries, especially Norway, Russia, Denmark, and Greece.

Europe is rich in minerals. It has a large supply of coal, which is used mainly to provide power to industries. Russia and Norway are Europe's major oil-producing countries. Other important minerals found in Europe include iron ore, lead, nickel, platinum, and zinc. Some northern countries, such as Sweden and Finland, specialize in producing timber.

Get This!

Many European crops are not native to the continent. Wheat, for example, came from Ethiopia in Africa. Oats came from China in Asia. Potatoes and tomatoes came from South America.

In Great Britain, only about 1 percent of employed individuals work in agriculture. In Albania, about 50 percent of employed people work as farmers.

German farmers harvest about 3.1 million tons (2.8 million metric tons) of rye each year.

Tourism

The tourism industry is very important to many European countries. This industry employs a large number of Europeans and brings money to local economies. France, Spain, Italy, Great Britain, and Germany rank among the world's most popular tourist destinations. Each year, for example, more than 75 million people visit France, more than 50 million come to Spain, and more than 40 million travel to Italy.

The continent's natural beauty is one of its major draws. Visitors enjoy sunny beaches along the French Riviera and Spain's Costa del Sol, on Greek islands, and at resorts along the Black Sea. Skiers head to the Alps or to one of Europe's many other mountain ranges. Other visitors enjoy the beauty of Great Britain's Lake District or take whale-watching trips in Norwegian waters.

The Eiffel Tower in Paris, France, receives about 7 million visitors per year. The tower, which is 1,063 feet (324 m) tall, consists of 18,000 metal parts held together by 2.5 million rivets.

The Rialto Bridge across the Grand Canal in Venice, Italy, was completed in 1591.

People who appreciate beautiful architecture often journey to Europe. Gothic cathedrals, which have pointed arches and high, curved ceilings, reach skyward in many French and German cities. Castles are found throughout the continent. In Moscow, the Kremlin was once a fortress protecting Russia's rulers from their enemies. Today, the Kremlin contains several museums, as well as the official home of Russia's president.

In Italy, Venice attracts many visitors with its canals and historic buildings. Other tourists visit the Netherlands to see fields of colorful tulips and windmills, or France to sit and watch the world go by from one of its sidewalk cafes. The Eiffel Tower, built for the 1889 World's Fair, attracts many people to Paris, the French capital.

With numerous churches and towers, Prague, the capital of the Czech Republic, is considered by many to be one of Eastern Europe's most beautiful cities. Another old and picturesque city is Koblenz, in Germany. Located on the Rhine River, its historic downtown was destroyed in World War II, but has since been restored.

When the 20th century began, the Netherlands had more than 10,000 working windmills. Today, more than 1,100 windmills remain in use.

Get This!

The Louvre Museum in Paris is one of Europe's oldest museums. It houses the *Mona Lisa*, a famous painting by the Italian artist Leonardo da Vinci.

Pompeii is an ancient Roman town. It was buried in ash after Mount Vesuvius, a nearby volcano, erupted in AD 79.

Many visitors marvel at Northern Ireland's Giant's Causeway. It is an **outcropping** of volcanic rocks that cooled into strange, six-sided columns.

The London Eye offers a great view of Great Britain's capital city and surrounding areas. About 3.5 million people per year pay to ride the observation wheel.

Industry

European industries benefit both from the continent's abundant natural resources and from Europe's highly skilled work force. Together, these strengths have made Europe one of the world's leading industrial centers. Industry in Western Europe is more developed than in Eastern Europe. Many countries in Western Europe use the latest technologies to produce huge quantities of goods. Other countries, especially those in Eastern Europe, tend to use older methods and manufacture fewer high-tech products.

Europe's industrial strength is not surprising, considering that modern industry originated in Europe. The **Industrial Revolution** began in Great Britain in the 1700s when new machines were developed to help grow crops, weave cloth, and produce energy. The main benefit of using machines was that more products could be made in less time and for less cost.

Factories in the Czech Republic produce streetcars, automobiles, and other vehicles.

Goods and Services

European manufactured goods and other products are found all over the world. Swiss watches and chocolate, French perfume and fashions, and English toffee are well known worldwide. Italy, France, and Spain are top producers of wine, while Spain, Italy, and Greece rank among world leaders in olive oil output. European manufacturers also produce goods such as medical drugs, synthetic rubber, steel, and fertilizers.

Services are also important to the European economy. Some of the world's largest banks are based in Great Britain, France, Germany, and Switzerland. Major **stock exchanges** are located in Amsterdam, Frankfurt, London, Paris, and the Swiss city of Zurich. Many European countries have large fleets of ships that carry goods to every part of the world. Many Europeans work in commerce, education, health care, and research.

Paris firms display their fanciest creations at Fashion Week shows in January and July.

Get This!

The Volkswagen automobile firm has its headquarters in Germany. The company name means "people's car." The company is widely known by its initials, VW.

The wealth of European countries varies widely. Oil-rich Norway, for example, produces more than $50,000 of goods and services per person each year. In Moldova, the figure is less than $4,000.

Europeans rank among the world's best-educated people. In nearly all European nations, more than 90 percent of the adult population can read and write.

Indigenous Peoples

People have lived in Europe for thousands of years. **Fossils**, tools, and other remains show that humans lived on the continent more than 700,000 years ago. One species, called the Neanderthals, lived between 130,000 and 35,000 years ago. These people are now extinct. Ancestors of modern humans first appeared in Europe at least 40,000 years ago.

In ancient times, humans in Europe lived in various tribes. These were small groups that searched the land for food. By about 6000 BC, people in southeastern Europe discovered they could grow food by farming and no longer needed to live as **nomads**. Their villages became Europe's first settlements. Basic farming methods spread to most of the rest of Europe by about 3000 BC. Later, **civilizations** began to grow around the Mediterranean and Aegean seas. The best known of these civilizations were those of ancient Greece and Rome.

Greeks in ancient Athens built the Parthenon between 447 and 432 BC. The Parthenon was a temple of the goddess Athena. Ancient Greece was strongest between 400 and 300 BC.

At the peak of its power, the Roman Empire included much of Europe, as well as parts of Asia and Africa. The empire gradually weakened after AD 200 and ended in 476.

Early peoples in Great Britain included the Angles, Celts, Danes, Jutes, and Saxons.

The Colosseum of ancient Rome opened in AD 80. The arena held crowds of 50,000 people or more.

The Age of Exploration

From the early 1300s to the late 1500s, Europe experienced the Renaissance. This was a period when Europeans became very interested in the arts and sciences. During this time, Europeans produced many new ideas, inventions, and works of art and literature. The Renaissance also brought improvements in methods of shipbuilding and sailing. These allowed European explorers to sail the world in hopes of finding a faster trade route to Asia. In Asia, ships could be loaded with valuable items such as spices and silk.

In the 1400s and early 1500s, Spanish and Portuguese explorers traveled farther than any Europeans had in the past. Vasco da Gama led the first voyage from Europe to reach India, by sailing around Africa. Christopher Columbus reached the Caribbean. Ferdinand Magellan led the first European round-the-world voyage, although he died before his crew completed the trip. Soon, explorers from many other European countries were making new discoveries. In 1497, John Cabot, sailing for Great Britain, became the first European to land on the North American mainland since the Vikings had traveled there centuries earlier.

Standing 197 feet (60 m) high in Barcelona, a monument to Christopher Columbus honors the Italian-born explorer who sailed for the king and queen of Spain.

Get This!

After the collapse of the Roman Empire, the Roman Catholic Church held most of the power throughout Europe. This period is known as the Middle Ages.

During the Middle Ages, Muslims from North Africa controlled much of Spain.

The Vikings were a seafaring people from **Scandinavia**. Some Vikings sailed from Europe to other continents.

From the late 1600s, the British town of Greenwich became an important center for astronomy, navigation, and timekeeping. The Prime Meridian passes through Greenwich. For many years, the world's time zones were based on Greenwich Mean Time.

Early Settlers

In many of the areas where Europeans explored, they started settlements. They established **colonies** in North America, Africa, and South America. European countries wanted colonies for many reasons. First, they could obtain natural resources and agricultural products, such as cotton, that European industries could then turn into manufactured goods. European countries sold these goods back to the colonies and earned profits. Colonists could also find and send valuable items such as beaver furs and gold to Europe for European use.

Europeans moved to the colonies for many reasons, too. Some Europeans wanted to bring the Christian religion to people in other lands. Others belonged to religious groups, such as the Huguenots, Quakers, Jews, and Moravians, that wanted to escape **persecution** in Europe. Some Europeans simply wanted free or inexpensive land, employment, and the hope of a better future.

In the 1500s, Spaniards built a settlement at Saint Augustine, Florida.

During the 1800s, Great Britain developed many colonies in Africa. British troops fought indigenous Zulu warriors in South Africa in 1879.

Over time, Europe came to rule a large portion of the non-European world. By the mid-1700s, India was under British control. Portugal ruled Brazil. Eventually, almost all of Africa and about one-third of Asia were colonized. In the 1500s and 1600s, the British, French, Spanish, Dutch, and Swedish began colonizing North America.

Under European colonial rule, many indigenous peoples were forced to change their ways of life. Men, women, and children were captured in West Africa and sent to other colonies as slaves. Many Native American peoples died from European diseases. Some civilizations, such as the Incas in South America, were completely destroyed by European settlers. The slave trade continued for centuries. Great Britain did not pass a law abolishing slavery in its colonies until 1833.

Today, people still **emigrate** from Europe to other countries around the world. Since the early 1800s, about 60 million people have left Europe. More than half of these people moved to the United States. In recent decades, tens of millions of people from other continents have moved to Europe. Many are attracted by Europe's need for workers. These people take jobs in areas such as the construction industry and health care.

The British social reformer William Wilberforce spent much of his life working against slavery. He successfully campaigned for bills that banned the slave trade and outlawed the keeping of slaves within the British Empire.

Get This!

Today, most former European colonies are independent countries. Some were willingly freed from European rule, while others had to fight for independence.

French colonies in North America were called New France. They included Canada and Acadia.

The Great Potato Famine occurred in Ireland between 1845 and 1852. The potato crop of 1845 was ruined by a fungus, and there was little other food. Many people died. Others left Ireland for North America and elsewhere.

Although some people willingly moved to colonies, others were sent against their wishes. These people included prisoners and orphans.

Population

About 740 million people live in Europe. In 1900, Europe was home to about one-quarter of the world's population. Today, only about one-ninth of Earth's population lives on the continent. Russia is home to more than 140 million people. More than 70 percent of them live in European Russia, which makes Russia the most populated country in Europe. Germany has more than 80 million people, and France, Great Britain, and Italy each have populations of more than 60 million.

Many people live in an area that stretches from the southern part of Great Britain through northern France and Germany to Moscow in Russia. Many more live in an area extending from Germany south to Italy. Tiny Monaco has one of the highest population densities, with about 30,000 people living on only 2 square miles (5.2 sq km) of land. Northern regions are much more sparsely populated. Iceland, for example, has only about 8 people per square mile (3.1 per sq km).

The largest city in Spain is Madrid, with a population of more than 3 million. Many people gather each evening at the Plaza Mayor, in the city center.

Monaco is located along the Mediterranean coast. French is the official language. Many people also speak a local language called Monegasque.

Politics and Government

For centuries, most European nations were ruled by kings, queens, and princes. Today, kings or queens still lead some countries, including Spain, Great Britain, Denmark, Norway, and Sweden. These countries are called monarchies. The monarchies are limited because citizens also elect officials to represent them in the government. Other countries are republics, in which all the officials are elected. Most European countries, both monarchies and republics, are **democracies**.

After World War II, many **communist** countries were established in Eastern Europe. The former Soviet Union and the former East Germany were two examples of communist countries. By the late 1980s, many people in these countries wanted more freedom. A large number of communist governments fell from power. In Berlin, the wall separating part of non-communist West Germany from communist East Germany was torn down, and the two halves of Germany were united.

During the 20th century, millions of Europeans were killed in World War I and World War II. After World War II ended in 1945, many Western Europeans worked hard to make the continent a more peaceful place. Today, many countries from all over Europe have joined the European Union. The countries have agreed to cooperate in areas such as trade, immigration, military policy, and human rights.

Get This!

Monaco is a monarchy. The Grimaldi family has ruled the country since 1297.

From 1932 to 1968, Portugal was a **dictatorship** ruled by Antonio Salazar. Today, the country has a democratic system.

Europe's newest country, Kosovo, became independent from Serbia in 2008.

Some European countries use a common currency called the euro.

The wall dividing Berlin stood from 1961 to 1989. Germans throughout Berlin celebrated when the wall came down in November 1989.

Cultural Groups

Europe is home to more than 150 cultural groups. In ancient times, vast stretches of mountains, forests, or marshlands separated European tribes. As a result, each group developed its own way of life. Many centuries later, groups such as the Basques of northern Spain continue to preserve their distinctive customs, traditions, religious practices, languages, and **dialects**.

Ideas that originated during the Roman Empire are still relevant today. Law, government, language, art, literature, medicine, and city planning are all areas influenced by ancient Rome.

About 50 languages and more than 100 dialects are spoken in Europe. In general, European languages can be divided into three main groups. Germanic languages include German, Swedish, and Icelandic. Romance languages include French, Spanish, and Italian. They came from the Latin language of the Roman Empire. Slavic languages developed in Europe's eastern and southeastern areas, as well as in Russia. They include Polish, Russian, and Bulgarian.

At Christmas, the Basques of Spain hold parades to honor Olentzero. According to Basque tradition, Olentzero brings toys and other gifts to children on Christmas Eve.

About 80 percent of Europeans are Christians. Many, particularly those in western and southwestern Europe, belong to the Catholic Church. Those in the east and southeast are generally Eastern Orthodox, while those in the north are generally Protestant. Many countries have their own national churches. For example, many Swedish Protestants belong to the Church of Sweden, and in Great Britain many Protestants are members of the Anglican Church. Europe also has about 40 million Muslims. Some of them have immigrated to Europe in recent decades.

Despite their different backgrounds, many Europeans consider themselves to belong to the country in which they live. Others think of themselves only as European. They take pride in the continent's exceptional history and its outstanding artistic, scientific, and political achievements.

Westminster Abbey in London was the setting for an Anglican Church ceremony in which Prince William of Great Britain married Catherine Middleton in 2011. The archbishop of Canterbury, who heads the Anglican Church, presided over the wedding.

Arts and Entertainment

Europeans have produced art since ancient times. The ancient Greeks and Romans built monuments that still stand today. They sculpted works of art, wrote books, and staged plays.

Many artistic movements that began in Europe have influenced artists around the world. The Spanish painter Pablo Picasso experimented with cubism, which reduces natural forms to basic shapes such as triangles, squares, and circles. Another Spaniard, Salvador Dalí, was a surrealist, painting dreamlike scenes that would not normally occur in the real world.

Many European musicians are also well known around the world. The world's first opera was performed in Italy in the 1590s. The symphony was developed in the late 1700s and early 1800s by European composers such as Joseph Haydn, Wolfgang Amadeus Mozart, and Ludwig van Beethoven. Modern music was pioneered by a Russian composer, Igor Stravinsky. Many jazz and rock composers have been influenced by his works, such as the *Rite of Spring*. European rock and pop stars since the 1960s have included the Beatles, the Rolling Stones, U2, Radiohead, Björk, and Adele.

Many of Pablo Picasso's paintings show people and objects from several different points of view, all at the same time.

The Beatles emerged from Great Britain in the 1960s to become the top-selling rock band ever.

One of Russia's major art forms is ballet. Russian dance companies include the world-famous Kirov Ballet of St. Petersburg and Moscow's Bolshoi Ballet. Spaniards enjoy flamenco dancing, which features clapping hands and stamping feet.

The great British playwright William Shakespeare wrote many comedies and tragedies that are still performed today. These include *A Midsummer Night's Dream*, *Romeo and Juliet*, *Hamlet*, and *Macbeth*. Other British writers have created lasting characters, such as Sir Arthur Conan Doyle's Sherlock Holmes and J. K. Rowling's Harry Potter. Great Britain has a very large film and television industry. Among the most admired directors in movie history are Ingmar Bergman of Sweden, François Truffaut of France, Pedro Almodóvar of Spain, and Werner Herzog of Germany.

The Kirov Ballet is well known for its performances of *Swan Lake,* with music by the 19th-century Russian composer Peter Ilyich Tchaikovsky.

The late-19th-century Dutch artist Vincent van Gogh produced about 900 paintings and 1,100 drawings in only 10 years.

When the German composer Johann Sebastian Bach died in 1750, few of his works had been published. Today, a complete recording of his works fills 172 CDs.

Dracula is a fictional character, but he may have been based on a real person. Prince Vlad Tepes ruled in Romania's Transylvania region in the 1400s. He committed many brutal murders.

Sports

The sport Americans call soccer is known as football in Europe. Football is Europe's most popular sport. It is the national sport of most European countries, and it is played on streets and in stadiums from Portugal to Russia. Professional and semi-professional teams play within their home countries and against other European nations. The best men's and women's teams compete in the World Cup tournaments, each of which takes place every four years.

Golf was developed in Scotland, which is part of Great Britain. The Honorable Company of Edinburgh Golfers, the world's first golfing club, was established in 1744. Amateur golfers enjoy the game across the continent, while professionals compete in tournaments such as the British Open.

Matthias Mayer is one of Austria's leading downhill skiers.

The American-born goalkeeper Karen Bardsley has starred for Swedish and British soccer teams in international competition.

Tennis is also popular with both amateur and professional athletes. On the professional tour, players compete in major tournaments. These include Wimbledon in Great Britain and the French Open in France. Other popular sports include ice hockey in Russia and Scandinavia, bullfighting in Spain and Portugal, rugby and cricket in Great Britain, and auto racing in Monaco.

Amateur athletes can take part in numerous sporting activities. Many Scandinavians own country cabins and enjoy winter sports such as skiing. Swedes take advantage of the country's many forests and lakes to camp, hike, and fish. Russians also fish, sometimes through holes in the ice on frozen lakes.

Skiing is a major attraction in the continent's many mountainous areas. Major ski resorts include Saint Moritz and Zermatt in Switzerland, and Innsbruck and Salzburg in Austria. Mountain rivers are used for whitewater rafting. Along the Mediterranean Sea, diving is popular, as are windsurfing and sailing.

Gleneagles, a hotel and resort in Scotland, has three championship golf courses.

Mapping Europe

We use many tools to interpret maps and to understand the locations of features such as cities, states, lakes, and rivers. The map below has many tools to help interpret information on the map of Europe.

COUNTRIES of Europe

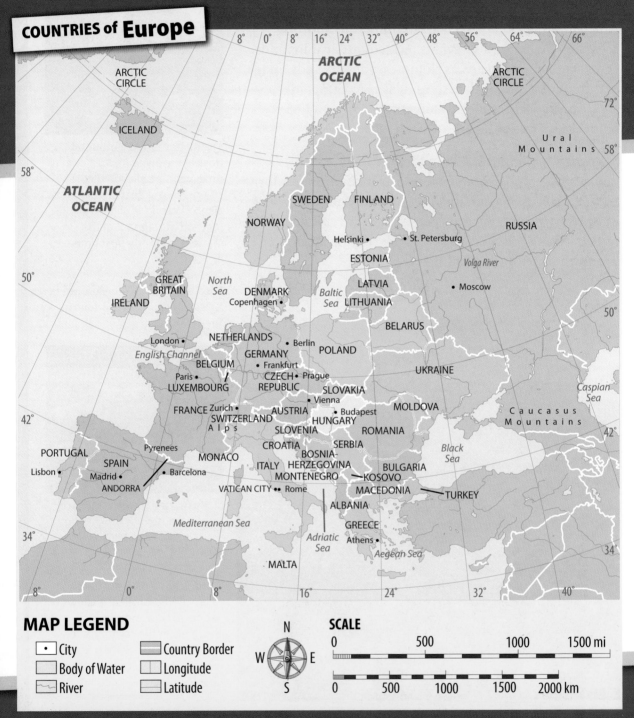

Mapping Tools

- The compass rose shows north, south, east, and west. The points in between represent northeast, northwest, southeast, and southwest.
- The map scale shows that the distances on a map represent much longer distances in real life. If you measure the distance between objects on a map, you can use the map scale to calculate the actual distance in miles or kilometers between those two points.

- The lines of latitude and longitude are long lines that appear on maps. The lines of latitude run east to west and measure how far north or south of the equator a place is located. The lines of longitude run north to south and measure how far east or west of the Prime Meridian a place is located. A location on a map can be found by using the two numbers where latitude and longitude meet. This number is called a coordinate and is written using degrees and direction. For example, the city of Los Angeles would be found at 34°N and 118°W on a map.

Map It!

Using the map and the appropriate tools, complete the activities below.

Locating with latitude and longitude
1. Which European country is found at 50°N and 32°E?
2. What body of water is located at 56°N and 4°E?
3. Which very large city is found on the map using the coordinates 48°N and 2°E?

Distances between points
4. Using the map scale and a ruler, calculate the approximate distance between the cities of Copenhagen and Rome.
5. Using the map scale and a ruler, find the approximate length of an airplane flight between London and Moscow.
6. Using the map scale and a ruler, find approximately how far north Finland extends above the Arctic Circle.

Map it yourself
7. Using latitude and longitude lines to guide you, write out the coordinates for the city of Madrid.
8. Find any two places on the map and calculate the actual distance between them using the map scale.

ANSWERS 1. Ukraine 2. North Sea 3. Paris 4. About 950 miles (1,530 km) 5. About 1,550 miles (2,500 km) 6. About 230 miles (370 km)

Quiz Time

Test your knowledge of Europe by answering these questions.

1 What continent is connected to Europe's eastern side?

2 What is the world's smallest country? How many people live there?

3 What is Europe's largest mammal?

4 What Russian fortress was built in Moscow?

5 Which famous tourist site in Paris was built for the 1889 World's Fair?

6 In what cities are Europe's major stock exchanges located?

7 How much of Africa did European countries colonize? How much of Asia?

8 What is a country called when a king or queen rules it?

9 What are Europe's three major language groups?

10 Who was a well-known British playwright?

ANSWERS 1. Asia 2. Vatican City; less than 1,000 3. The European bison 4. The Kremlin 5. The Eiffel Tower 6. Amsterdam, Frankfurt, London, Paris, and Zurich 7. Almost all; about one-third 8. A monarchy 9. Germanic, Romance, Slavic 10. William Shakespeare

Key Words

civilizations patterns of culture and society that developed in specific regions, nations, or groups

colonies places where foreigners settle that are then governed by their home country

communist a type of government in which everything is supposed to be held in common by the people but, in practice, is controlled by the state

democracies countries where people have equal rights and vote to choose government officials

dialects local forms of a language spoken in specific regions

dictatorship a system of government in which the leaders hold complete power

diversity having a large variety

emigrate to leave one's country of origin to move to another country

endangered at risk of extinction

extinct no longer existing

fossils preserved remains or traces of things that lived a long time ago

Industrial Revolution a period in the 1700s and 1800s when powerful machines and large-scale factory work were developed

medieval related to the Middle Ages, a period in European history that followed the fall of the Roman Empire in the fifth century

nomads people with no permanent home who survive by moving from place to place

outcropping one or more rocks that stick out from the surface of the soil

peat a fuel that comes from partly decayed plants

persecution harsh or cruel treatment, often based on racial or religious hatred

plateaus broad, flat areas of high land

Prime Meridian the line of 0° from which east and west longitudes are measured

Scandinavia an area of northern Europe that includes Norway, Sweden, Denmark, Finland, Iceland, and the Faroe Islands

steppes treeless plains

stock exchanges places where people meet to buy and sell shares of companies

tundra a vast, treeless, mostly level plain in the Arctic region

Index

Log on to www.av2books.com

AV[2] by Weigl brings you media enhanced books that support active learning. Go to www.av2books.com, and enter the special code found on page 2 of this book. You will gain access to enriched and enhanced content that supplements and complements this book. Content includes video, audio, weblinks, quizzes, a slide show, and activities.

Audio
Listen to sections of the book read aloud.

Video
Watch informative video clips.

Embedded Weblinks
Gain additional information for research.

Try This!
Complete activities and hands-on experiments.

WHAT'S ONLINE?

Try This!	Embedded Weblinks	Video	EXTRA FEATURES
Create a timeline of Europe. Write a biography about a notable European. Decide where you would go on a trip to Europe. Completing a matching activity on European statistics.	Find out more about Europe. Learn more about European history. Explore a European landmark. Discover some of the animals that live in Europe. Learn more about some of the art found in Europe.	Watch a video about European cultures. Take a tour of a city in Europe.	**Audio** Listen to sections of the book read aloud. **Key Words** Study vocabulary, and complete a matching word activity. **Slide Show** View images and captions, and prepare a presentation. **Quizzes** Test your knowledge.

AV[2] was built to bridge the gap between print and digital. We encourage you to tell us what you like and what you want to see in the future.
Sign up to be an AV[2] Ambassador at www.av2books.com/ambassador.

Due to the dynamic nature of the Internet, some of the URLs and activities provided as part of AV[2] by Weigl may have changed or ceased to exist. AV[2] by Weigl accepts no responsibility for any such changes. All media enhanced books are regularly monitored to update addresses and sites in a timely manner. Contact AV[2] by Weigl at 1-866-649-3445 or av2books@weigl.com with any questions, comments, or feedback.